Beckwourth

by Mark Weston

Single copies of plays are sold for reading purposes only. The copying or duplicating of a play, or any part of play, by hand or by any other process, is an infringement of the copyright. Such infringement will be vigorously prosecuted.

Baker's Plays
c/o Samuel French, Inc.
45 West 25th Street
New York, NY 10010
bakersplays.com

NOTICE

This book is offered for sale at the price quoted only on the understanding that, if any additional copies of the whole or any part are necessary for its production, such additional copies will be purchased. The attention of all purchasers is directed to the following: this work is fully protected under the copyright laws of the United States of America, the British Commonwealth, including Canada, and all other countries of the Copyright Union. Violations of the Copyright Law are punishable by fine or imprisonment, or both. The copying or duplication of this work or any part of this work, by hand or by any process, is an infringement of the copyright and will be vigorously prosecuted.

This play may not be produced by amateurs or professionals for public or private performance without first submitting application for performing rights. Licensing fees are due on all performances whether for charity or gain, or whether admission is charged or not. Since performance of this play without the payment of the licensing fee renders anybody participating liable to severe penalties imposed by the law, anybody acting in this play should be sure, before doing so, that the licensing fee has been paid. Professional rights, reading rights, radio broadcasting, television and all mechanical rights, etc. are strictly reserved. Application for performing rights should be made directly to BAKER'S PLAYS.

No one shall commit or authorize any act or omission by which the copyright of, or the right to copyright, this play may be impaired. No one shall make any changes in this play for the purpose of production.

Publication of this play does not imply availability for performance. Both amateurs and professionals considering a production are strongly advised in their own interest to apply to Baker's Plays for written permission before starting rehearsals, advertising, or booking a theatre.

Whenever the play is produced, the author's name must be carried in all publicity, advertising and programs. Also, the following notice must appear on all printed programs, "Produced by special arrangement with Baker's Plays."

Licensing fees for BECKWOURTH are based on a per performance rate and payable one week in advance of the production.

Please consult the Baker's Plays website at www.bakersplays.com or our current print catalogue for up to date licensing fee information.

Copyright © 2005 by Mark Weston
Made in U.S.A.
All rights reserved.

BECKWOURTH
ISBN **978-0-87440-257-5**
#1796-B

For his invaluable encouragement and support,
I gratefully dedicate *BECKWOURTH* to Mr. Gordon Parks

Author Notes:

This play may be done as either a one-man performance, or a cast may be used for the various roles...while Jim Beckwourth's character narrates.

(The following optional opening may be used in lieu of, or in addition to the scripted opening of the play.)

>*(An actor appears on stage, sitting and putting on makeup and his costume as he addresses the audience:)*
>
>**NARRATOR.** I'm wondering if anything has changed since I was s student. Like for instance, what are you learning? No, I'm not going to lecture or give a test. In school I learned who discovered America...and who was the first president...and who invented the electric light. I'll bet you also knew, like me, who hit the most home runs...and who was the best basketball player. But, you know, it wasn't till recently that I found out about a man I never knew existed. No, I didn't learn about him in school...or on T.V...or even in the papers. He never was a president, general, or ever dunked a basketball. When I was invited here I kept thinking about when I was your age—why I never knew anything about him...although he did a lot to open up this country.
>
>*(HE rises and moves downstage...as **J**IM **B**ECKWOURTH.)*

BECKWOURTH

(SETTING: LECTURE HALL)

(TIME: 1855)

(The stage is barren except for a chair and a table. Before the entrance of JIM BECKWOURTH, Indian chants accompanied by drums are heard. JIM enters. He is dressed in the garb of a mountain man of the 1830's. Beaver hat...buckskin jacket, pants, and wearing a silver dollar on a chain around his neck. He is carrying a long rifle. JIM eyes the audience, removes his hat, nods and moves to center stage. He listens to the chants until they stop. [JIM's dialogue can be spoken as it as in the 1800's. For instance: "you" could be "y'", "my" could be "m'", "often" as "offen", etc.])

JIM. Evening folks. My name's Jim Beckwourth!

*(**HE** stares at the audience, incredulously putting them on.)*

Never heard of Jim Beckwourth or what I did? Well, that doesn't surprise me none. But soon that'll be taken care of. Some men who hardly raised a finger for America, got their names on the lips of everyone. Tain't right. It's why I'm here! I'm a mountain man. We ain't no different than you...mebbe a little meaner...dirtier... independent. For that's what it takes t' survive. Most of us...only got ourselves to make sure we make it from one day to the next.

*(**HE** lifts his rifle.)*

This here's m' Hawken rifle. *(Aims it at the audience.)* Don't worry, it ain't loaded. Pretty thing. Weighs about 12 pounds...low sight, set trigger with a percussion lock. All the mountain men swore by the Hawken. Can stop a chargin' buffalo in it's tracks. Been with me mebbe 30 years. Bought it off of a trapper during a *Rendezvous*. Figure you don't know what that is.... Well, it's kinda like a holiday or a get-together where mountain men meet...sell their skins to the fur company...buy their provisions for the comin' season...sit around and swap tales...wonderin' whether they'll all be together the next summer.

Like my clothes? Been wearin' skins like these since I first went west. Maybe not so fine...but skins 're skins and so long as they keep you warm in the winter and cool in the summer...then that's all that's important.

You're lookin' more surprised then a mean old grizzly starin' at a scrawny polecat trying to steal its grub. I never seen a mountain woman...and you never heard of a black mountain man...even though I did as much if not more than Daniel Boone or Lewis or Clark to open up this country.

Looks to me you have your doubts. I reckon if I was white my name might be legend by now. If Daniel Boone was born black, do you think you might've heard of him? I doubt it.

(Looks up proudly) I'll tell you somethin'...you're lookin' at an Indian chief! That's right...I'm Jim Beckwourth, a chief of the Crows! Still doubting me? I got me a story if you'd like to hear it. Well, since I see you all still hangin' on to your seats...I figger we'll spend time together. *(Sits, carefully placing the rifle on his lap.)*

I've been spendin' time with T. D. Bonner. He's a book writer. Sitting among you. He's kinda shy so I won't bother to point him out. Mr. Bonner's writin' my life story.

A lot of folks been sayin' I tell nothin' but lies. That's human nature for you. But I always say, unless you were there...and saw otherwise...then you don't know. What I told Mr. Bonner, and what you're about to hear—its true...so help me God!

(Starts polishing his rifle.)

I was born in Virginia, on April 26, 1798, and was raised in a little Missouri town called Saint Charles...some twenty miles or so north of Saint Louis. My pa was Jennings Beckwourth...my ma's name was Miss Kill. He was white...and owned her when they was in Virginia. In the late 1790's pa gave up his plantation and settled in Missouri...so's that they could live together in peace. Even in Missouri they could never marry...but it didn't matter much because they were more married than those who were. And so that's the way they made their way. But for as long as I can remember I wanted none of it! I had a wild streak that got me in heaps of trouble. My problem was that I couldn't live like a nigger in the white man's world. So, I made up my mind that I was gonna be somebody, someday.

It really all started when I was workin' as a blacksmith's apprentice in Saint Louis. *(**HE** places the rifle against the wall and takes a moment to reminisce.)* Saint Louis, now that was a city even then! Parked on the Mississippi river, like it was a door to the west. Most of the townsfolk were God-fearin'. These were the ones who brung the only idea of eastern culture to the town.

The ladies, they wore long dresses, some made of satin, bonnets and usually carried somethin' they called a parasol. *(Imitating a woman:)* So's to keep the sun out of our eyes. *(As **J**IM)* Tickles me when I think of a squaw carryin' one of them. The Saint Louie gents wore stovepipe hats, satin vests and high collars...and covered the air with their fancy odors.

Then there were the mountain men, either comin' from or goin' west. Now they were somethin'. With beards down to their chests and over their shoulders...carryin' their long rifles and their haul of beaver pelts. They smelled of firewood and animal...and sweat! They were my heroes! Exceptin' for Moses Black Harris who was one of the meanest, most ornery creatures on earth. He could handle a tomahawk better than any Injun. Think I'm exaggeratin'? Then go ask a Blackfoot, Sioux, or even a Cheyenne. He always smelled fierce. I don't think he bathed more than once a year. But I'll get back to him later.

> (JIM *pantomimes walking a horse to his blacksmith workbench and prepares a hoof for a new shoe.*)

In the summer of 1815, I was workin' as an apprentice to a Mr. Casner who owned a blacksmith shop. One day I was shoein' a horse for a mountain man named Kennerley. He was in his 40's, and had been goin' west for almost ten years. He was some six-foot tall and built like he was a blacksmith hisself. I knew that when the time came he'd be a match for any animal or human. He used to run his fingers through his bushy blonde hair and talk and talk, and talk....

KENNERLEY. Boy, there's nothing like sleeping on a riverbank with the stars flickering like fireflies from one horizon t' the other. Y'r always lookin' forward t' the new day...never knowin' whether you'll hit pay dirt or lose your life tryin'. But all the time bein' certain it was gonna be excitin'.

JIM. *(NARRATIVE)* When I got a mountain man's horse t' shod...it took me longer, 'cause I couldn' hear enough of their stories. I asked him about dealin' with Injuns....

KENNERLEY. There ain't no hard rule on dealin' with 'em...but don' expect too much..."

JIM. *(AGE 17)* Y' mean they're lazy?

KENNERLEY. Not lazy, son. Proud! They're fightin' for their own survival in any way they know...whether it's stealin', scalpin' or usin' their friendship to an advantage.

JIM. Well, I wouldn' deal with 'em!

KENNERLEY. *(Laughs)* Then it's a good thing you ain' a trapper...for y' wouldn' last.

JIM. Mr. Kennerley, I'd be willin' t' do just about anything t' join y'. I want t' see the places you've seen...'n get t' do the things you've done.

KENNERLEY. Ain' no place for a boy. 'Specially a city fella.

JIM. *(NARRATIVE)* The forge was giving off a heat that made the summer day like an inferno. *(JIM demonstrates proudly and forcefully.)* Well, I raised up my hammer and bent a piece of hot steel on the first blow....

KENNERLEY. *(Impressed)* Ooee! You're mighty handy with that hammer, boy. If you're hankerin' for a new life jes' report t' General Johnson's company on the wharf by the end of the week. We're lookin' t' bargain with the Sac and Foxes for the use of their lead mines up north. Bring a good shootin' iron...a bed roll...'n your freeman papers. Tell 'em I sent you.

JIM. *(NARRATIVE)* Just then old man Casner come in with Moses Black Harris. Casner was in his fifties and looked like he never missed a meal in his life....

CASNER. Still not through, boy? *(HE scratches his backside.)* I got a good mind t' get me another helper who ain' so lazy.
KENNERLEY. The boy didn' do nothin'...t'were my fault.
CASNER. He's worthless. Niggers are all alike. I got me a good mind t' take a whip t him!
JIM. I ain't your slave...you lard-ass piss ant!

JIM. *(Demonstrates, reliving the moment.)* *(NARRATIVE)* Casner threw a hammer at me...and missed. I threw and hit him with the same hammer on his knee. Well he let out a holler and hit the floor like a crippled bear....

(JIM, as CASNER falls to the floor.)

CASNER. You're through y' miserable bastard! Y'r father c'n have y'.

JIM. *(NARRATIVE)* Well, I just threw off my apron... *(Throws off imaginary apron.)* And said to Kennerley, "I'll be seein' y'." 'N took off. Casner weren't through with me. A Constable came to my lodgin's sayin' I stole items from the blacksmith shop...which weren't true. It was Casner trying to even the score. The Constable saw it my way...least he had sense enough not to try to stop me. Well, *(grins)* I mean he had only one arm. "'N I had a loaded .44! T'weren't no contest. I headed for the wharf. Casner and the Constable took me off'n a keelboat I was hidin' on, and brung me back to Saint Charles in the mornin'.

Pa was furious. He took me t' the woodshed, closed the door 'n give me a thrashin'. Well, not really... *(Enjoying the memory, acting it out with zest.)* I cried 'n hollered...while he kept strikin' leather on some hides. Guess it satisfied Casner 'n the officer. When they left, me 'n Pa had a talk....

    JIM. Who am I, Pa?
    JENNINGS. What kind of question is that? You're my son.
    JIM. Then why don't I have family? I mean like everyone else? Why can't me and Ma accompany y' when y' visit your kin? Ma tell me y' both come from Virginia. She says y' quit y'r homestead t' be with her.
    JENNINGS. It doesn't matter.
    JIM. It matters t' me, Pa. You say I'm your son but others say I belong t' you. I'm confused. Been that way since I c'n remember. 'N it pains me.
    JENNINGS. Don't pay no mind to them, Jim.
    JIM. But they never let up. So I figure, since they won't accept me as an equal, then I've got to make my own way...in any way I see fit.
    JENNINGS. I hate to hear you talk this way. Your ma and I figured to see you as a fine blacksmith. A smithy would always be accepted regardless of the color of his skin. And now...?
    JIM. But I want more than that. I want to be looked up to...by everyone. Some day I'm going to walk the streets of Saint Lou...and people'll move aside and I'll hear them sayin'..."There goes Jim Beckwourth...ain't he somethin'?
    JENNINGS. You're dreaming son. And I can't blame you...but we all can't have what we want.
    JIM. Why?
    JENNINGS. Because we all have responsibilities.

JIM. To who?

JENNINGS. A wife…a family…a home. I still may be able to square things with Mister Casner.

JIM. No, Pa…he hates my kind! I'll never go back to him…or to anyone. Pa, m' insides cry out whenever I think of goin' west…or hear tales the trappers tell.

JENNINGS. Do they tell you what it is to go hungry for days? Freezing in the winter without even a fire to keep you warm? Having no one to care for you when you're sick…give you a decent burial when you die?

JIM. *(NARRATIVE)* But there was nothin' he could say that'd change my mind. *(JIM lifts a silver dollar hanging around his neck.)* He give me this silver dollar piece which he once wore around his neck. Ma cried. But she knew I had to have m' dream…so she kissed and hugged me and wished me well. Ma and Pa was holdin' each other as they watched me leave. I don' figure they'd ever be apart—here on earth…or forever.

(Goes downstage.)

I skedaddled down to the Mississippi wharf ag'in and joined General Johnson. We headed to the Sac and Fox Indian lead mines, in northwest Illinois. Kennerley took me under his wing.

(The lights dim. The blue of night and fog from the river appear. Sounds of the river, frogs, crickets and Indian drums and chants are heard.)

One night on the river a mountain man said he saw an Injun on the bank. I hit the deck…. *(HE falls to the floor and aims his rifle.)* and shook all the while I aimed m' rifle. I looked up at Kennerley…

JIM. Injuns?
KENNERLEY. Not necessarily. Hostiles aren't known for givin' warnings.
JIM. Then how d' you know when they're there?

KENNERLEY. Well...y' use your Injun sense.
JIM. What's that?
KENNERLEY. It's what y' acquire...if'n they let you live long enough.

(Lights are restored.)

JIM. *(NARRATIVE)* A few days later, I saw more Indians than I thought ever existed. General Johnson parlayed and made a deal with them over the use of their lead mines. I worked near on two years as a blacksmith and hunter. Made friends with the tribe, 'n they taught me plenty, like how t' stalk game, find y'r way 'n survive if'n y' get lost 'n even trap the beaver. M' pa always said, "People are people no matter who they are. Treat 'em like y'd want t' be treated 'n y' won' have much trouble." 'N he was right!

When I come back t' Saint Lou in 1821, I was thinkin' 'bout buying a stove pipe hat 'n fancy shirts...but St. Lou wasn't ready for that. Instead, I had me some store bought clothes and still looked like a proper gent. Got it all 'ceptin for the scented water. I weren't ready for that yet. 'N Ma 'n Pa were impressed. It felt good bein' different. But the townsfolk still hardly paid me no mind. But it didn't matter none, 'cause I got hired as a trapper with the Ashley Rocky Mountain fur company.

I was finally headin' west. Not many Negroes could say that in those days.

(JIM pantomimes mounting a mule. The plains are projected on the rear screen. Sounds of mules traveling west. A harmonica is heard.)

The trek out to the plains took months...through dust clouds and under the scorchin' rays of the sun. My body was covered with sweat and grime...every so often I'd look over my shoulder at the trail, takin' me perhaps forever from the life I had known. But that didn't last long...because my mind was made up that I wasn't comin' back till I got what I come for.

(The French song "Aupres de ma blonde" is heard. The sounds of the mules and harmonica stop.)

Our first stop was to be Ashley's camp that he left behind on his last expedition. It was jus' east of the Rockies...which meant we still had a long and hard road t' travel.

A lot of French-Canadian trappers joined us. Baptiste was one of 'em. He was a scrawny sixteen-year old orphan who signed on as a apprentice mule skinner. Moses Black Harris didn't take long in making him his personal slave.

One night at an encampment, Kennerley and I admired a blade hangin' from Baptiste's belt....

    JIM. *(AGE 24)* Never seen a blade like it. Right, Kennerley?
    KENNERLEY. Never, Jim. Whatcha want for it, son?
    BAPTISTE. *Mon père!*
    KENNERLEY. How about this shiny gold piece?
    BAPTISTE. *Merci, Monsieur Kennerley...mais...c'est impossible...mon père me l'a donné!*
    KENNERLEY. *Ou est votre père?*
    BAPTISTE. *Il est mort. Ma mère aussi.*
    JIM. What's he say?
    KENNERLEY. His pa gave it to him.
    JIM. Where's his father?
    KENNERLEY. The boy's an orphan.

    JIM. *(NARRATIVE)* Just then Harris stood over Baptiste....

    HARRIS. Boy, fetch me some more bread and grub! Be quick about it!
    JIM. Why don't you get it yourself ol' man. You're no cripple.
    HARRIS. I wasn' talkin' t' you! *(To **BAPTISTE**)* Move, boy!
    BAPTISTE. *Oui, monsieur.*

*(**H**ARRIS and **J**IM stare menacingly at each other, until **B**APTISTE returns.)*

JIM.   Give it here, Baptiste.

*(**J**IM spits on the plate.)*

JIM.   *(NARRATIVE)*   Harris come at me with his knife, like a madman. He cut my arm. I kept dodgin' Harris' thrusts…without a knife of my own, it was all I could do.

*(Choreographed, **J**IM acts out the fight.)*

Slash…slash…he kept coming at me…all the time swearin' he was gonna cut my heart out. The men kept hollerin' for Harris t' finish me off.

(Sounds of men egging them on.)

I kept retreatin'…it weren't a fair fight…but I learned that there weren't any rules with mountain men. Baptiste called…"Monsieur, Jeem!" 'n threw me his knife. When Harris saw it, he stopped in his tracks. I crocked my bleeding arm, then slowly flicked the knife from side to side. I forced him back into a campfire. He felt the heat 'n made a rush. I side-stepped and hit him atop his head with the heavy handle. We circled each other…parried, then Harris rushed me again, tripped 'n crashed t' the ground. Like a cat, I pointed m' knife at his throat. The men hollered f'r me to stick 'em!….

JIM.   Harris., y' bastard! Y" goin' t' leave the young 'un alone?
HARRIS.   Yo!
JIM.   Agin!
HARRIS.   Yo!
JIM.   And that goes for all of y'…y' leave him alone, y' hear?
ASHLEY.   Drop that knife, Jim!

(JIM tosses knife to the ground.)

ASHLEY. You're new here, Jim. You're eager and you're going to need watching. I can't spare any men for that. And I won't tolerate your slicing up my best trapper. Greenhorns like you are worthless.
KENNERLEY. T'weren't his fault, General.
ASHLEY. This doesn't concern you, Kennerley. Heed me, Jim, another incident like this and you'll be walking back to Saint Louis. Is that understood?
JIM. Yes, sir.

JIM. *(NARRATIVE)* When things quieted down, Baptiste put his bedroll next to Kennerley's and mine. He offered me the knife. Kennerley let Baptiste know what I was sayin'....

JIM. Put it away, Baptiste, you'll be strong enough soon.
KENNERLEY. *Laisse-le, Baptiste, bientôt tu seras fort.*
JIM. Besides, it'll help the men t' think twice before they bother y' again.
KENNERLEY. *A de plus il les aidera a penser avant d'agir.*
JIM. It's just not right for a man or boy…made to do another's chores.
KENNERLEY. *Ce n'est pas bien pour un homme ou un enfant…de faire le travail d'un autre.*

JIM. *(NARRATIVE)* Well, we finally reached General Ashley's old camp. Never seen such a poor lot of mountain men. They were starvin' 'n cold 'n told stories 'bout bein' attacked by Cheyenne…'n losin' all their horses 'n a lot of men.

Snow covered the territory 'n game was almost impossible to come by. I led a huntin' party, 'n brought back enough game t' feed the lot of 'em by usin' the Injun sense I learned from the Sac and Foxes. Don't think mountain men could've survived without buffalo meet 'n their hides, which we used for clothes 'n t' drape over bent wood, 'n cottonwood poles, t' make bull boats. *(Laughs)* The General learnt he weren't dealin' with a greenhorn. Puttin' down the beast weren't so simple…'specially when it's wounded. Well, while with the hunting party the General took a shot at a hefty bull, but it hit too low. The animal put its head down and charged General Ashley, who didn't have time t' reload.

(Sound of a charging and snorting bull is heard. JIM aims his rifle.)

Well, I aimed m' Hawken 'n put a ball behind its shoulders.... It fell less than five feet from sendin' the General t' his grave. He was grateful....

ASHLEY. Jim, I think you're ready to lead your own brigade.
JIM. I appreciate your trust in me, general, but you're lookin' for a more experienced man. I hardly trapped before...this here's the furthest I've ever been. I'm just not ready.
ASHLEY. Is that your mind?
JIM. Yes, sir. Most of the men in camp are more deservin'.

JIM. *(NARRATIVE)* The next day General Ashley asked for a volunteer t' join Harris who was goin' t' bargain with the Pawnees for horses. The men weren't too happy with the prospect of joinin' him....

MAN. What happen to Jim Kelly?
SECOND MAN. Y'r a mean son of a bitch, Harris!
THIRD MAN. I wouldn' trust him far as I can spit!
ASHLEY. Gentlemen, since there's no volunteer, we'll have to draw for one.
JIM. It won't be necessary, General. I'll go if y' give me leave t' speak t' him.

JIM. *(NARRATIVE)* I took Harris aside...but kept m' distance downwind!....

JIM. The men here call y' great leg for turning your back on them when they're in need. So, I want you t' bear one thing in mind.
HARRIS. What's that?

JIM. If I should give out and you choose to leave me t'perish...if I have the strength to raise and cock m' rifle...I'll stop y' dead in your tracks.

HARRIS. Jim, then I propose you go ahead of me at your own pace. If I direct the path and give you the lead, it'll be your own fault if you tire out. Then it's every man for himself.

JIM. *(NARRATIVE)* It was Jake with me. 'Cept that Moses still had another six months before his next bath. It took us ten days t' reach the Pawnee village...but by then they were gone. It's the way of the Indian t' keep movin' with the buffalo. Harris figured they headed for their winter quarters. We were movin' along till a blizzard hit.

(Sounds of a howling snowstorm and wolves are heard. Lights dim to a blue wash as wind blows across JIM's face.)

The trails were now covered with deep snow, our only choice for survival was t' head for Ely's trading post, mebbe five miles north, slowin' us up. The storm took its toll on Harris. We could barely make a mile a day, even with our snowshoes. Our provisions were almost gone, 'cept for the carcass of a scrawny deer....

JIM. Harris, there ain' much time. If I leave now I should reach Ely's post right after sundown.

HARRIS. *(Pleading pitifully)* Jim, don't leave me here t' die!

JIM. Don't move none, so I can find you.

HARRIS. No, Jim! Come back...come back...don't leave me. Don't leave me!

JIM. *(NARRATIVE)* I gave him my blanket, fed the fire, then took off. The snow was so deep, and the wind so fierce, each step of the way became a test of endurance.

(Pantomimes the trek.)

My eyebrows were icicles, and my mouth felt like it was frozen solid. All I knew was if I even stopped for a spell...I'd be a dead man. But there was just so far a human being can push himself...and I couldn't go on no more...I'd fall...get up...then fall again...

*(**HE** falls to the floor.)*

...and finally jus' lay there.

(Looks up from the floor.)

Didn' know becomin' famous was gonna be this much trouble.

(His head drops...then raises.)

The next thing I know's a couple of Injuns are liftin' me...and makin' me run t' get m' circulation back. They give me some gruel...while all the time I kept pointin' 'n sayin'..."Moses Harris...Moses!"

Mebbe they were Hebrews from the lost tribe 'cause they finally understood. We all headed back t' where Harris lay half-alive 'n still moanin' for me t' come back.

(The sound of the snowstorm ends.)

The men at Ely's tradin' post couldn' believe their eyes when me 'n Harris were carried in by the Injuns. They were rewarded. The next thing I remember, I was in a bed covered with blankets before a roarin' fire. Ely said, me 'n Harris had been sleepin' for close to three days. Well, m' pa never said it was gonna be easy. The most important thing was that I was a mountain man...and alive.

Me 'n Harris made contact with the Pawnee 'n bargained for enough horses t' carry Ashley's company over the Rockies and into beaver country.

(Rear projection of the Rockies.)

We left the Pawnee, met the main troop, 'n headed for the Rockies. We couldn' make more than three or four miles a day. The December snows, the rivers and the need t' keep huntin' wasn't easy even for a mountain man. Finally we kept movin' up hill…knowin' we were getting' near the Great Divide. I was the first t' reach the peak. I dropped the reins on m' pack mule 'n horse…chopped a hole in a frozen creek with m' axe, 'n saw the water runnin' downhill…goin' west. We made it! I threw my hat in the air 'n hollered, "YAHOO!" The men below all knew what I meant, 'n started yellin' themselves hoarse. Whiskey poured, men wrestled in the snow and danced to a mouth organ.

(JIM dances wildly to the tune of a harmonica.)

Ever hear a drunken harmonica player? Even the mountain goats held their ears. Things quieted down as we all stood 'n saw what looked like millions of buffalo grazin' below. Mebbe there were half as many 'cause I think we were all seein' double at the time.

The column started the trek down the divide in good spirits. Some thought we oughta go back up the mountain 'n celebrate again. But Ashley said the bar was closed!

If'n y'ever plan on climbin' the divide, look at the biggest boulder up there, 'n y'll find m' initials carved on it…'n have one on me.

(End of rear screen projection.)

A month later we was settled in our camp on the Green river. The men were issued their beaver traps, guns, ammunition, coffee, flour, tobacco 'n jugs of whiskey. Now don' start thinkin' we were all a bunch of drunks. We jus' liked fire with our water. The General told us…

ASHLEY. Gentlemen, we will divide into brigades with six men in each brigade. You'll all take separate routes and I'll expect to meet you all again right here for Rendezvous around the first week of July.

JIM. *(NARRATIVE)* We all knew how important it was to take care of our traps, because without 'em our trip west would've been for nothin'. We were usin' Newhouse traps.

(Pantomimes demonstrating the trap.)

The jaws have a curve and can hold any beaver no matter what size. They cost $10.50 apiece. We worked in pairs...one t' set the trap 'n bait it with castoreum which were the sex glands of the beaver......the other t' drive the stake and keep guard. Each team was responsible for skinnin' 'n storin' the pelts. I was lucky t' draw Clyman as a partner, 'cause he was a good teacher 'n about the best beaver trapper in the west. Baptiste 'n Harris drew each other...'n there was no trouble. Everything was fine. The men tied their skins into plews...that's twelve skins tied t'gether 'n stashed in a hole. Natcherly we had a map tellin' us where t' find 'em on our way back t' *Rendezvous*.

(Sinister drums are heard.)

One night in March, the brigade was in camp preparin' our pelts when we had visitors. Mebbe a dozen Arapaho. They come as friends, so we give 'em grub 'n tobacco, n' they left peacefully. But that night they come back, only this time they come for our scalps. One hostile tried t' grab m' rifle, but I took it from him 'n clubbed him with the butt. Then I scattered the fire ashes with it as the Injuns hid in the brush 'n opened fire. We searched the woods 'n figgered they were gone. When we got back t' camp...we found Moses Black Harris...with a tomahawk in his scalp.

We knew it was time t' break camp 'n skedaddle. Didn' even have time t' bury Harris. It was jus' like Pa said, "Mountain men don' expec' nothin'. It's the way they choose t' live."

(End of Indian drums.)

We kept settin' our traps in new creeks, cacheing the plews, 'n keepin' our eyes open for hostiles. We did have a few more skirmishes but lived t' tell 'bout 'em.

Clyman finally figgered it was time t' start fetchin' our caches 'n headin' for *Rendezvous*. It was too bad since the beaver were comin' in like locusts. But with the weather getting' warmer, the new pelts were too lean 'n won't be worth nothin'. Besides, Clyman didn' want t' hold the general up from headin' for St. Lou before the end of summer.

(The sound of mountain man music is heard. Lights lower and a campfire flickers.)

The *Rendezvous*, which was also known as the 'Fair of the Mountains,' stretched for miles 'n was jus' as Kennerley tol' me when I was Casner's apprentice. Trappers 'n Injuns come ridin' in with their fur packs from all over the territory. We'd see old friends, sing, gamble, hold shootin' matches, race our favorite horses, hunt…'n some would spend all they made without a thought. The whiskey flowed , music played, we all danced…or at least tried to…'n got into mean fights. There was grub aplenty…'n enough Injun women for all. Some men lost their wives when others took a fancy to another man's wife. It's the way it were.

(Lights and sound slowly diminish.)

Ashley was sorry t' hear 'bout Harris' departure. We never remembered the bad things about a departed mountain man…only the good things he'd done. T'weren't easy with Harris.

One night the General and I had a talk....

ASHLEY. We'll be heading east in a few days. I'd like you to join us.

JIM. If you don' mind, General, I'd just as soon remain here. I still ain' got what I come for.

ASHLEY. If that's your mind, Jim I'll get Kennerley to replace you.

JIM. General, if it pleases y', I'm ready t' lead m' own brigade.

ASHLEY. You've earned the honor. You may form your brigade after I make the announcement in the morning.

JIM. General, there's something else I'd like to ask of you.

ASHLEY. What's that?

JIM. Will y' look in on m' ma 'n pa?

ASHLEY. Rest assured, Jim

JIM. *(NARRATIVE)* Me 'n Kennerley had us a talk. I knew he was thinkin' 'bout leavin' but hoped he'd change his mind....

JIM. Sure wish y' were goin' with me. Ah hear the Great Salt Lake's real beaver country.

KENNERLEY. Even so. Gonna miss y' Jim Reckon it' be awhile before we meet again.

JIM. Y'll be back.

KENNERLEY. Naw, Jim...m' rheumatism's been getting worse. Jus' had too many years of huntin' 'n wadin' in icy streams—tryin' t' stay alive.

JIM. Never figgered t' hear y' t' talk like that.

KENNERLEY. It's jus' piper time. Ahm done...it's your country now, Jim...respect it...and you'll do jus' fine.

JIM. *(NARRATIVE)* It was like sayin' goodbye t' a father. I cried t' see him wavin' as he led Ashley's train...goin' east. I watched Baptiste ride out with the train. For a long spell he'd look straight ahead, 'cause he knew I talked Ashley into taking him back...but then far in the clearin' I saw him turn...'n nod. I was sad to see the boy go...but I knew that where I was headin' 'n the plans I had, the chances of survivin' were less than none...especially for a young boy like Baptiste.

I reached the Great Salt Lake in early November. Log cabins were standin' at the foot of the Wasatch mountains, close by the Great Salt Lake. Mebbe six hundred mountain men 'n peaceful Snake Indians were encamped. Among the trappers was Jedediah Strong Smith. If there ever was a legend mountain man...it was Jedediah. His middle name summed him up perfect. He once had his head in a bear's jaws 'n lived t' tell about it. Well, he tol' me...m' name was known all the way out there. C'n y' imagine, the great Jedediah Strong Smith treated me like an equal. Well, why not? Wasn't I becomin' one of the best mountain men around?

We holed up in our cabins for awhile 'n then moved out for another season of beaver trappin'. I led m'own brigade. Couldn' believe how beautiful the canyons 'n peaks 'n streams were. We hauled in the biggest cache of beaver skins ever. I can tell you General Ashley was impressed at the next *Rendezvous*....

ASHLEY. Jim, when you first came west with me, I thought you were trouble. But I was wrong.
JIM. Didn' mean to be a bother, General.
ASHLEY. I'm aware of that now, Jim. I've never seen better or more beaver pelts in all my days.
JIM. I found 'em north of the Snake!
ASHLEY. That's Blackfoot territory. It's too dangerous.
JIM. I have t' do what I have t' do, General. Besides, I used m' Injun sense.
ASHLEY. *(Laughs)* And you're getting to act and look more like an Indian than a mountain man.
JIM. I expect to do a lot better.
ASHLEY. I'm sure you shall. However, I regret that I'll never see it.
JIM. What're y' sayin', General?
ASHLEY. I'm selling out to Jacob Astor. My family and I owe you a great deal, Jim Not only for saving my life, but also for being such a fine example for the trappers...and contributing so much to the company and the nation's growth and prosperity.

JIM. Thank you, General. But what would y' be doin' with yourself?

ASHLEY. I'm planning on returning to politics. I intend to run for Congress.

JIM. I'd vote for you...if I could.

ASHLEY. Perhaps someday. Meanwhile, the Ashleys offer you the hospitality of our home, forever.

JIM. *(NARRATIVE)* Can you imagine what the slavers would do if they saw a Negro havin' tea with the general? It could bring on a civil war...or at least a few riots. But I weren't lookin' t' upset people. I only wanted m' due.

Ashley said m' folks were fine 'n were proud t' hear 'bout my success...it pleased me plenty!

One night at the *Rendezvous*, we were all sittin' around a fire when grubby Ol' Caleb Greenwood, who had no teeth, 'n was short, white-haired 'n was always spittin', kept spinnin' his tales...'bout how he escaped from a whole Commanche war party. One mountain man said, "Hell, Caleb, I did too!"....

CALEB. Mebbe so, but y'd never escaped the Crow! *(spits)* Jim's the only one among y' the Crow would let live. *(spits)*

JIM. Caleb Greenwood y're a crazy ol' man.

CALEB. Ol, mebbe, *(spits)* but not loco. I live with the Crow. They like t' hear stories 'bout men who c'n fight 'n are brave. I made up one 'bout you bein' one of their own. *(spits)* Y' have to understand that Injuns are jus' like children... *(spits)* they believe most everything they hear. I tol' them that y' was kidnapped by the Blackfoot when y' was a baby. 'N then they sold y' t' the whites f'r an indenture. *(spits)* When they heered that...they set up a-hootin' 'n a-hollerin'...musta lasted a week! I tol' them y' was comin' back 'n that y've killed many of the Crow's worst enemy... *(spits)* the Blackfoot!

JIM. 'N they bought it?

CALEB. They're waitin' f'r you, Jim

JIM. I can't speak Crow.

CALEB. I'll learn y'.

JIM. How would they know me?

CALEB. I tol' 'em they c'n tell it was you by the silver dollar y' wear 'round y'r neck. *(spits)* They're on the look out.

JIM. Well...they can keep on lookin'. M' future's in Saint Lou.

CALEB. *(Slaps his thighs, laughs and goes into a brief dance.)* Mine was too!

(End of crackling fire sound.)

JIM. *(NARRATIVE)* At the end of *Rendezvous*, I said m' *adieu*s to the General 'n me 'n Jedediah 'n a few other trappers made our way t' Crow territory. Montana! It was the farthest north I'd ever been. Caleb had taught me Crow 'n I kept mullin' over how mebbe I c'n get the tribe t' helpin' me. Sure, already made some money, but figgered if'n the Crow were willin', mebbe it'd be comin' in faster....

(The sound of wolves howling...bears roaring...a fast moving stream are heard.)

JIM. Jed, I'm goin' up stream 'n set some fresh traps.

JED. *(HE looks up at the sky.)* I don't think it's wise, Jim There ain't much sun left.

JIM. I'll be back before dark. Save me some grub.

JIM. *(NARRATIVE)* I never got t' enjoy m' supper. Because from atop a rise, Jedediah figgered he saw the last of me. I was bein' escorted by a Crow war party as a prisoner back t' their village. Before long all the mountain men knew that Beckwourth had gone under.

(Removes his shirt, and is bare chested.)

'n y' say I got took on purpose...well, you're right. It was time I made m' move. Somehow, sooner or later, I knew it'd work out...one way or t' other. 'nd what d' ya think I made sure they saw?

(Displays his silver dollar from around his neck.)

Y'r right again...m' silver dollar.

The Crow call themselves Absaroke...Bird People. They got t' hollerin' abou[t] 'n pointin' at the dollar, jus' like Caleb said they would. And I sure was gratef[ul] he kept his promise of teachin' me Crow.

Big Bowl, a tall, battle-scarred, solidly built chief around his fifties, tol' th[e] members of his council that they'd know for sure 'bout me if some ol' Cro[w] woman who lost children years ago could prove I was her son. Well, the[y] pawed 'n stared at me till one ol' woman who was one of Big Bowl's wive[s] says that her son had a mole over his left eye.

(JIM stares at audience, grins, and draws down his left eyelid.)

And there it was. Far as they were concerned...I come home.

Big Bowl took me as his own son 'n give me the name of Morning Star. H[e] told the tribe that Caleb's words were true, 'n that their enemies will tremb[le] at my hands. I was bathed by four of m' sisters 'n dressed in fine Cro[w] garments. Figgered I shoulda got caught sooner.

Big Bowl 'n me had ourselves a private talk....

(The conversation includes Indian sign language.)

    JIM. My father, the white man has big canoes that travel up and dow[n] rivers without wind or paddles.
    BIG BOWL. Then how do they move?
    JIM. Steam...'n engines.
    BIG BOWL. Engines?
    JIM. It's like when y' boil water...the steam is harnessed 'n makes th[e] boat move.

BIG BOWL. What else did you learn?

JIM. They have guns that speak with thunder...so strong...one hundred braves would fall at a time.

BIG BOWL. *(Concerned)* Where do they keep them?

JIM. M' father has nothing to fear. The white man only uses them when he's at war. He is at peace with the Crow.

BIG BOWL. Caleb speaks of tipis that laugh at the great winds. Of iron horses...of much corn...

JIM. He speaks the truth!

BIG BOWL. I know. My son are you in need of a wife? A brave must have a wife from another brave's lodge.

JIM. *(NARRATIVE)* I got me a pick of four women. The one I chose was named Still-Water. She was the eldest of the four 'n the prettiest. They tol' me she was a good provider 'n would make me happy. A warrior rode through the village like a town crier, beatin' on a small drum, 'n announcin' to the tribe about our comin' wedding. Still-Water followed me to the ceremonial site.

People think that Indian men led the women out of disrespect. T'weren't nothin' of the kind. It was the husband's way of breakin' the trail in summer and winter, 'n protectin' them from harm.

Still-Water 'n me stood before the tribe 'n had our thumbs cut slightly. Then our thumbs were tied together so's our blood mingled. The ceremonial head stood over us....

CEREMONIAL HEAD. Morning Star...and Still-Water...you're now one, just as your blood is one.

JIM. *(NARRATIVE)* Still-Water waited for me in a tipi covered with buffalo hides. When I opened the tipi flap...I see her lyin' on a bear rug, wearin' the bridal dress she'd been preparin' since she become a woman. Three giggling Crow women left the tipi, while I got down on m' knees 'n faced m' bride.

Still-Water was as pretty a bride as you'd want t' see...long hair, soft skin 'n a body that most men dream about. I knew that if I was ever goin' t' get what I come for...I'd have to make some sacrifices 'n compromises. *(Winks, laughs)*

Liked m' weddin' night so much...I figgered t' have me a lot more of 'em.

Soon I was joinin' war parties....

> *(JIM applies war paint in pantomime to his face, as war chants are heard.)*

One of m' first how-de-do's was with a mess of Blackfoot.

> *(Displays a lance.)*

This here's a type of lance usually carried by the chief of the war party. It shows his rank and is also used t' order his men into battle. Well I see the chief point the lance so I charge the Blackfoot. The Crows are a little slow 'n catchin' up t' me, so I'm alone in takin' on the Blackfoot.

> *(Pantomimes fighting the Blackfoot.)*

I puts one down then starts on another. The Crow finished their charge 'n withdraw. But when they see me still fightin' hand t' hand...they charge again...'n this time they stay around till the Blackfoot are beat'n. I scalped m' first Blackfoot, then relieved the unlucky bastard of his gun, war club, bow 'n quiver of arrows. When we got back t' the village...the war party spread the word of what I did. Big Bowl 'n Still-Water were especially proud of their son and husband.

It's a Crow custom that when a son draws the first blood of the enemy, his father must give away all his property to the village. Big Bowl was broke...but happy. He was the father of a brave. Were the other Crow fathers envious? Not on your life. Envy is a quality unknown to the Crow. Back east, envy warps the mind and ruins the lives of so many. Bein' a Crow wasn't all that bad. They made a lot of sense.

M' next war party was a big one of ninety braves.

(Sound of gunfire.)

One mornin' we come 'cross a wagon train bein' attacked by Blackfoot. The whites musta thought they were gonners when they see m' braves comin' at 'em. But they held their fire long enough t' see us tear into and chase the Blackfoot. The whites were glad t' see us...'n surprised t' learn that Jim Beckwourth was fightin' with a Crow war party....

WAGON MASTER. Jim, I c'n tell y' that once they find out about this in the east you're gonna be as famous as Lewis and Clark.

JIM. *(NARRATIVE)* So I figgered the word should be getting out. In short order I was gathering me a load of *coups*. That's another thing that needs explaining.

A *coup* is the Injun way of giving credit to a brave who does a gallant act. If a brave just touches an enemy without payin' with his life he earns a *coup*. I heered of an Injun getting his *coup* by tyin' a rock t' a rope, settin' it down from above a sleepin' enemy 'n touchin' him with the rock. On the other hand, if an Injun is a coward...he's treated like an outcast.

One of m' *coups* made me a chief!

For months I had joined war parties 'n come back with glory 'n plenny o' *coups*. Big Bowl gave me the name of Antelope...the first to attack. He said I deserved t' carry a lance 'n lead m'own war party. Shucks, I could've tol' him that.

M' war party was made up mostly of young, inexperienced braves, 'n m' brother-in-law Black Panther. We brung back the biggest haul of horses the Crow had ever seen. We returned to the village with our faces covered in black paint signifyin' a great victory. Well, there was celebratin' the likes of which I hadn't seen since my last *Rendezvous*.

(Tom-toms are heard.)

Arapoosah, who was the big chief of the Crow give me m' new name...Is Ko Chu-E-Chor-e which in Crow means, The Enemy of Horses. Oh, by the way by then I had me seven wives...but Still-Water was still chief of m' lodge.

It warn't till two years later that I got me the chance t' make my move t' getting my fortune. The Crow had a tradin' agreement with John Jacob Astor's American Fur Company. I often asked about joinin' the Crow as they delivered our animal hides t' the tradin' post...but Arapoosah 'n the Crow council turned me down....

JIM. *(AGE 31)* Arapoosah, I've been with you for many moons, led war praties t' far off lands 'n returned. Why would I leave my many wives, horses...'n the love and respect of my father, brothers, and of all the Crow...t' live in the white man's world?

ARAPOOSAH. You speak too much of leaving. You have spent too many moons with the white man. Does their spell still hold you?

JIM. I serve the Crow! My brothers, for years the white men've cheated us all! They are not our friends. The fur company never gave us the full value of our hides. I have lived with the white man 'n can speak their tongue. I promise t' come back with a better deal...and with more than cloth. I'll bring more and better guns.

JIM. *(NARRATIVE)* They finally saw it my way. Figgered when I get back east...I'd become a politician...seein' how I c'n win people over. Even without a firearm...or a knife.

Early fall, we arrived at Jacob Astor's trading post. I see how difficult it was for my brothers t' make themselves understood t' the proprietor, Mr. Kipp....

JIM. Mr. Kipp, none of them understands English. They want scarlet cloth.
KIPP. You there...who taught you English?
JIM. What matters is what I'm here for. You've robbed the Crow 'n me for the last time.
KIPP. What are you talking about?
JIM. If I tell e'm the truth about how little we got for all the work we've done, this here post won't be standin' much longer.
KIPP. What do you want, mister?
JIM. The name's Jim Beckwourth...and I'm askin' for a better deal for m' friends 'n me.
KIPP. Jim Beckwourth? You worked for General Ashley. What are you doing with the Crow?
JIM. It's a long story.
KIPP. Why don't you sup with me, tonight? I think we might work out a deal.

(JIM reads contract.)

JIM. For a promise of makin' sure the Crow don't find out how they'd been cheated...'n assurin' the fur company that the pelts'll be coming...I'm to be put on salary for arrangin' exclusive trading rights with the Crow and a bonus for plews delivered above the quota.

(Looks up at KIPP.)

My own plews would be bought at a premium price?
KIPP. Agreed!
JIM. The Crow trust me.

KIPP. And business is business. Jim, you're not a Crow...you're living in two worlds. You're going to be a very rich man. Sure will help get you what you said you came west for. So what's your decision?

JIM. *(Shakes hands with KIPP.)* Mr. Kipp, y' can tell Mr. Astor he hired himself another fortune. Who knows? I may be buildin' a new mansion next to his! *(Laughs)*

JIM. *(NARRATIVE)* The Great Spirit didn' take long t' let me know how he felt....

> *(Sounds of war whoops and weapons firing are heard. JIM releases an anguished Indian cry.)*

JIM. ALAPEE! WHAT HAVE I DONE?

> *(The sky is red with fire flickering.)*

JIM. *(NARRATIVE)* When the tradin' party got back t' the village it was burnin'. We saw the smoke a distance away 'n come tearin' in at a gallop. We saw our people lyin' dead, our lodges burnin' 'n women mournin' for the slain. I headed for m' wives lodges. By a miracle, Still-Water's lodge was untouched.

> *(The sky remains red but the flickering stops.)*

I came just in time t' see m' son born. Big Bowl tol' me the Blackfoot struck at dawn that day. They butchered women, children and ran off with many horses. Still-Water tol' me they killed m' other wives 'n children and her brother Black Panther. She begged me to avenge his death and wash the tribe's faces. She showed me m' baby. I figgered it was Black Panther returned.

> *(Rear projection of daylight.)*

I joined Arapoosah's war party of over two hundred braves. We found the Blackfoot settin' atop a tall granite wall which was built like a fort. It wasn't going to be easy to take. Some of our braves tried a frontal attack but were driven back with heavy losses. Arapoosah figgered that the Blackfoot were takin' too many Crow lives 'n ordered them to withdraw....

JIM. Arapoosah...tell your warriors t' follow me! Let them use the rifles I brought them...and I'll show you how the braves of the Great White Chief fight their enemies.

(JIM raises his lance and leads the attack.)

JIM. *(NARRATIVE)* I ordered another frontal attack. While the Blackfoot were fightin' these braves, I had another group scale the wall from the rear. They didn't know what hit 'em 'n when the fightin' was all over...not a Blackfoot was left alive. Crows died too...includin' Arapoosah!

Months later at a council lodge, all the prophets 'n elders, elected me t' be Medicine Calf, one of the head chiefs of the nation. Well, I stayed a chief for close t' six years. M' St. Louie bank account was full up from the American Fur Company's deposits. The Crow followed me...'n did exactly as I tol' 'em. I was really thinkin' of ending m' life there...

Comin back from trappin' I come into the village 'n see m' braves stumblin' 'n fallin' 'n acting like drunken fools. They tol' me that Kipp gave them whiskey. He now lived in the fur company's lodge in the village....

JIM. Kipp, I want you out before sundown!
KIPP. *(Laughs)* Sorry, Jim, I have to stay put. The fur company told me to replace you.
JIM. Why?
KIPP. They feel that lately the Crow've been too busy taking to the warpath instead of trapping. Astor's looking for more pelts...not scalps.
JIM. I'll talk to them.

KIPP. Won't do you no good. His mind is made up.

JIM. You can confine an Injun to a steady life for just so long...'n now the fur company plans t' take hold of the tribe with their rot! T'weren't in our agreement.

KIPP. We'll do what we have to do. Nothing or no one'll make a difference. You're through here, Jim.

JIM. *(NARRATIVE)* It was time t' take stock. If the tribe won't listen t' me, then m' time was growin' short, 'n I didn't want to witness how the tribe would suffer.

Red Fox, a young trouble-makin' brave came t m' lodge with a mob of other braves 'n stood before me with a raised battle axe....

RED FOX. Medicine Calf, you've cheated the Crow. We won't follow you. The tribe will follow Red Fox!

JIM. Red Fox, lower your battle axe 'cause there won't be no fightin'. The white man has brought his poison t' the Crow. He will turn brother against brother till only the buzzards'll be left to mourn. The Crow've disobeyed me. I won't stay around to see the nation become weak and fleein' from their enemies and our women and children made slaves. Keep your battle axe ready Red Fox, for you're gonna be needin' it soon. My brothers, I'll move my lodge to across the river. Warriors...I'm done.

JIM. *(NARRATIVE)* I spoke to Still-Water in m' lodge....

JIM. Still-Water raise Black Panther well, for one day he will be chief.

(JIM lifts BLACK PANTHER and kisses him.)

Black Panther you know that I love y'...'n the Crow...but I have to leave.

(Sounds of horses.)

JIM. *(NARRATIVE)* Crows rode out a-ways with me...and finally one by one they took their leave. The last I remember was seein' Still-Water holdin' m' son 'n watchin' me until I rode out of sight. I felt an empty feelin' in m' stomach. Turnin' away from the tribe that meant so much to me was painful. But I still had a dream to come true. I'm gonna walk the streets of St. Lou...'n people'll move aside...'n I'm gonna hear them sayin'... "There goes Jim Beckwourth...ain' he somethin'!"....

(Daylight, St. Louis pier. A steamboat whistle is heard. JIM is looking down from a boat railing.)

JIM. (AGE 36) Look at the crowds! Musta been waitin' f'r hours...'n come from miles around t' see the Crow chief. Well, they sure won' be disappointed. Don' see m' folks anywhere. Didn' want 'em t' miss it. It's just the way I expected. Well, I shouldn' keep 'em waitin'.

(JIM leaves the steamboat, and walks the streets of St. Louis in his Indian garb.)

(Bows to a woman) Howdy, ma'am. *(Bows to a gentleman)* Afternoon, sir. It's me...Jim Beckwourth...I'm back! *(**HE** looks disappointed as no one returns his greeting. **HE** approaches others)* Y' lookin' for Jim Beckwourth? Well here I am! *(Spreads his arms out, and watches as they leave, paying no attention to him)* I'm back! Aincha interested in meetin' the Crow chief y' heard so much about?

SHERIFF. Whatcha doin' on the street, nigger?

JIM. I'm Jim Beckwourth!

SHERIFF. Yeah, and I'm Sheriff! Y' know y'r place. The sidewalk's f'r white folk. Now git t' where y' belong.

JIM. *(NARRATIVE)* This time the odds were in the law's favor. I mean, now I was facin' a man with both arms, and his loaded .44! .... *(**HE** walks away, confused, and heads for General Ashley's home. Knocks on door as street noise fades out.)*

JIM. Howdy, is General Ashley at home?
HOUSE SERVANT. What're you doin' here?
JIM. I asked if General Ashley's at home.
HOUSE SERVANT. This ain' no place for a darkie!
JIM. I'm Jim Beckwourth!
HOUSE SERVANT. I'm warnin' you! The congressman'll have y'r hide! Now you move on, nigger, before I take a stick t' y'!
JIM. *(Grabs **HOUSE SERVANT** by the throat)* Call me, Mr. Beckwourth! Y" hear? Mr. Beckwourth!
ASHLEY. What is the meaning of this? Release him! This instant!

(JIM releases his grip)

Who are you? What are you doing here?
JIM. Don't you know me, General?
ASHLEY. Jim?
JIM. Yes, sir.
ASHLEY. My God, I never thought I'd ever see you again. Come into the parlor.

(Restore general lighting.)

The word was that you were dead, and then that you were with the Crow.

JIM. *(NARRATIVE)* I told Congressman Ashley m' whole story from the time Jedediah saw me taken away by the Crow t' my arrivin' in St. Lou, 'n still bein' treated as a nigger!...

JIM. Congressman Ashley, sir…all my life I've wanted to be somebody…I swore there'd be a day when people'll accept me for what I am…spent years as a mountain man…led the Crow against their enemies…became a Medicine Calf…made plenny of money…and here I am back in St. Lou' and nothin's changed.

ASHLEY. Jim you expected too much from people who don't know what you've done...and are not interested in finding out. You've returned from a world where the color of a man's skin isn't important.

JIM. Suppose you're right...then there's nothin' left for me but to see my folks.

ASHLEY. They're buried in St. Charles'.

JIM. When?

ASHLEY. Within the last few years. I'm sorry.

JIM. Then it was all a waste.

ASHLEY. I disagree. You've made a name for yourself, Jim, only you've been looking for acceptance from those who don't give a damn. You just never realized you got what you were looking for from the Crow and the mountain men.

JIM. *(NARRATIVE)* His words kinda opened my eyes. There's a lot more to my story, like when I saved Colonel Zachary Taylor's life in the Florida swamps against the Seminoles. *(Laughs)* Guess you could say he couldn've become president without me...or how I fought in the Mexican War as a scout for General Winfield Scott...or helped General Kearney liberate California...but it'll have to keep for another time...or at least till Mr. Bonner's book is published.

Did y' know I've got a town 'n peak named after me? Yup, in California. When y' get home, look up a map. It's about sixty miles north of Sacramento. And while you're about it...give a look some forty miles east of Beckwourth Peak 'n my pass. It was the pass I found which let the pioneers get into and settle California 'n even dig for gold.

Yep, there's a lot more...but it'll have to keep. Now, even after all these years, it's like I never left St. Charles. Mebbe someday m' name'll be in all the books, 'n remembered by people for years to come.

Well, I suppose it's time for us to go our way. Seems I'm always sayin' hello 'n goodbye t' folk. But before I skedaddle…I'll leave y' with a mountain man wish…I hope we all meet again…

(Raises his rifle above his head.)

…at Rendezvous!

CURTAIN

Also by
Mark Weston...

101 Winning Monologues for Young Performers

Beckwourth: the Later Years

Winning Monologues from the Beginnings Workshop (with Peter Sklar)

Please visit our website **bakersplays.com** for complete descriptions and licensing information.

OTHER TITLES AVAILABLE FROM BAKER'S PLAYS

BECKWOURTH: THE LATER YEARS

Mark Weston

Historical / 1m, Optional Ensemble cast up to 15

Frontiersman, scout, James P. Beckwourth is credited with discovering the accessible route into northern California in the 1800's, known today as the "Beckwourth Pass." Named a chief of the Crow Nation, Jim Beckwourth's many feats and accomplishments have gone largely unsung in American history. Who among us grew up reading about the "black Daniel Boone?" A wonderful immersion into the life and character of one of America's best, told with wit, honesty, and great story-telling style. By making obscure but important history come alive, this play is a good vehicle for school touring or a way to introduce history in a novel way to classes. By the co-author of the very popular *WINNING MONOLOGUES FROM THE BEGINNINGS WORKSHOP* as seen on the Bravo television and *BECKWOURTH*.

BAKERSPLAYS.COM

OTHER TITLES AVAILABLE FROM BAKER'S PLAYS

101 WINNING MONOLOGUES FOR YOUNG PERFORMERS

Mark Weston

101 Winning Monologues for Young Performers Including 101 valuable acting hints!

Acting teacher Mark Weston has written a companion to his most successful *Winning Monologues from the Beginnings Workshop*. After observing his acting students over many years struggling with books that offered speeches and recitations in lieu of monologues, Mr. Weston wrote his true and original monologues for young performers. He is pleased to acknowledge that many young performers have benefitted. For the first time, 101 short, precise and valuable acting hints are included, deriving from his successful acting career and including direct quotes from his teacher Lee Strasberg. These monologues can be a big help for young people beginning to study and audition for careers in theatre, film or TV.

www.ingramcontent.com/pod-product-compliance
Lightning Source LLC
Chambersburg PA
CBHW072339300426
44109CB00042B/1950